40 DAYS TO life-changing ›› FAMILY WORSHIP

15 MINUTES A DAY COULD CHANGE YOUR HOME LIFE

MYRON EDMONDS

Forty Days to Life-Changing Family Worship
Copyright © 2012 by Spirit Reign Communications & MyRon P. Edmonds. All rights reserved.

BLUEPRINTS
GRAPHIC DESIGN & WEB DEVELOPMENT

Cover and interior layout design by Ornan Anthony of OA.Blueprints, LLC
Visit OA.Blueprints' exciting website at www.oablueprints.com

Edited by: David Robinson

No part of this publication may be reproduced, stored in a retrieval system, or transmitted, in any form or by any means, electronic, mechanical, photocopying, recording, or otherwise, without the prior written permission of the copyright holder.

Printed in the United States of America

ISBN: 978-0-9856400-2-6

SPIRIT REIGN PUBLISHING
A DIVISION OF SPIRIT REIGN COMMUNICATIONS

*Matt & Leo
So glad we
connected!
We family now!
#CLE*

PRESENTED TO THE _____ **FAMILY**

BY _____

DATE _____

▶ WARNING!

Reading and applying the contents of this book could cause the following:
- An invasion of God's presence
- A blessed family
- A revived marriage
- Saved children
- Miracles
- The out pouring of the Holy Spirit in your home.

Proceed with caution

Dedication

To my wife, Shaneé, who exemplifies the life-changing love of God everyday to me.

To my daughter, Teylor, whose artistic expression and beauty constantly remind me of God's love.

To my son, Camden, whose lively personality personifies adventure and hope.

To my parents, Ronald and Phyllis Edmonds, for making family worship a life-changing experience for me and inspiring this book.

I am also grateful for my siblings Edward, Letetia, Corey, and Yolanda for their love and support.

Acknowledgements

Michael and Angela Brown; for your unselfish blessing that made this book a reality. The seeds you've sown will reap a harvest in everyone's lives who reads this book. You guys are awesome!

Pastor John Coaxum; for pressing me to get the book done. I needed your motivation.

Pastor Stephen P. Ruff; for being the voice of truth in my life. You are "major" baby!

My accountability partners: Seth Yelorda, Vandeon Griffin, Debleaire Snell, Alfonzo Green, Joel Kibble, Wesley Knight, and Eric Thomas for not accepting my tendency to procrastinate. Without you brothers I would utterly fall.

The Glenville SDA Church; for trusting me to be your leader and helping me in the formation of this idea.

SECTION 1: LAYING THE FOUNDATION

Introduction: *A Life-Changing Idea*...*xiii*

    CHAPTER 1: My Story..1

    CHAPTER 2: The Purpose...5

    CHAPTER 3: The Problem..7

    CHAPTER 4: 2 Powerful Ideas...11

    CHAPTER 5: The Solution: When God Shows Up...13

    CHAPTER 6: Does God Feel at Home?..17

SECTION 2: BUILDING THE FRAMEWORK

    CHAPTER 7: What is Family Worship?..21

    CHAPTER 8: Getting Started: My Attitude...23

    CHAPTER 9: Getting Started: The Components..27

    CHAPTER 10: 7 Benefits..33

    CHAPTER 11: The Ten Commandments of Family Worship.......................................37

CHAPTER 12: Where and When..41

CHAPTER 13: The Power of 40..43

CHAPTER 14: For Maximum Results..45

SECTION 3: 40 DAY CHALLENGE

Week 1 - "Feeling Good" - Family Closeness...51

Week 2 - "Words Matter" - Words of Affirmation...................................59

Week 3 - "We Need Healing" - Family Healing..67

Week 4 - "What is Our Family Vision?" - Family Vision..........................75

Week 5 - "We Have a Ministry" - Family Ministry...................................83

Week 6 - "A Family that Prays" - Family Prayer..91

A FINAL WORD

What Did God Do in Your House...99

{ x }

Section 1: Laying The Foundation

Unless the Lord builds the house, the builders labor in vain.

Psalm 127:1 NLT

A LIFE-CHANGING IDEA

I want to inspire you to think big for your family. You need to see a vision of what your home life can be versus what is. I want to introduce to you a paradigm shift to family worship that has the possibility of changing your family life.

What if…
- Family worship was more than just a religious exercise and actually became life-changing?
- Family members experienced God in *every* family worship?
- Family members made decisions for Christ in family worship?
- Parents could lead their children to the Lord at home?
- Family curses and strongholds were broken?
- Marriages were healed?
- Impossible situations became possible through the power of intercession?
- Prodigal children came home?

It's not a far-fetched idea. I know it can happen and I know that God desires for His people to experience His life-changing presence every time we come before Him. It's a simple attitude adjustment and approach that you have to make when you bring your family together. You are simply saying, "God I expect you to move in our time together in a powerful way because You promised it." The Bible gives us a promise for all of God's people including families when He says, *"Again I say to you that if two of you agree on earth concerning anything that they ask, it will be done for them by My Father in heaven. For where two or three are gathered together in My name, I am there in the midst of them."* [1] This is what we are expecting every time we come before Him as a family. We can expect answers to prayer through His presence when we come in His name. This is what family worship should be about. We need to change the mindset that church is only reserved for the weekend. The power of the church experience should be in our homes everyday. I believe that the presence of God in its fullness can be experienced in our homes everyday if we make household worship a priority. What's so awesome about this concept is that God wants to be with you. He is not standing aloof waiting for your family to come to Him, rather the scripture gives us this picture, Jesus says: "Here I am! I stand at the door and knock. If anyone hears my voice and opens the door, I will come in… " [2] Isn't that a mind blowing thought the God of the universe wants to literally come in your home? I have often wondered what it would be like if the President of the United States paid a visit to my home. Sounds exciting. But someone greater than the President wants to live with you and bless you. God wants to be apart of your family. He wants to do " exceedingly, abundantly, above and beyond what you could ever imagine or think." [3] All we have to do is let Him in through the door of family worship.

While you read this book, my prayer that you will be motivated and inspired to make the lifestyle commitment to bring your family together consistently to worship God. If you are ready to experience God like never before in your home then keep reading, if not put the book down. Are you ready? Lets go!

Chapter 1
MY STORY

As a child, we had family worship almost every day. Many times my father would wake us up at 5 in the morning! However, it wasn't the regularity that made the difference in my life, it was how the worships were planned and approached. The emphasis in my home was the quality of worship versus quantity of worship. My most memorable and life-changing spiritual experiences as a child in a Christian home weren't primarily at church, but at home during family worship. Our family worship was so dynamic that it met the spiritual needs of all ages. It was never monotonous or ritualistic, and most of all; it was FUN!

It's almost like some churches you attend. Some have church and others have church. In some churches, they pray, sing, and even preach about Jesus, but no matter how sincere the congregation, boring worship is boring worship. Worship should not only inform, but it should also inspire. Jesus said, "Yet a time is coming and has now come when the true worshipers will worship the Father in the Spirit and in truth, for they are the kind of worshipers the Father seeks. God is spirit, and his worshipers must worship in the Spirit and in truth." [4] Information that is not balanced with inspiration only appeals to the head but not the heart.

{ 1 }

On the other hand, a church where the worship connects with an audience will inspire people to make changes in their lives. If worship doesn't move us to action then it isn't true worship. True worship always moves the worshipper to action.

As a good church approaches an engaging worship, so should a family. There must be an intentional effort not just to say, "we had worship" but to rather, "worship made a difference in my life." It must connect to the head and the heart. Consider how much of an impact church worship services have on your life and compare that to daily family worship. You'll begin to see the life-changing potential that family worship has on the faith development in families. The truth is family worship is not important to us anymore. It is no longer a priority on our to-do list and often gets bumped because of other, less-important activities.

Our spiritual development is important. If we don't view family worship as indispensable as our church attendance, we will remain one-day-a-week Christians. Worship must become part of the family lifestyle. Just because family worship is in your home doesn't mean it is less significant or less holy. If there ever was a worship experience that should be powerful and life-changing it should be in the place where we spend so much of our time with the people we love the most.

In my childhood home, and even now with my own family, our family worship is based on three principles that will revolutionize your family worship time:

Chapter ONE: My Story

(1) Connecting to God
(2) Connecting to each other
(3) Expecting God to act

In any worship setting, worship practices become routine and monotonous when our focus drifts from God to ourselves. At this point showing up becomes more important than God showing up. What inevitably happens is many of us go in and out of worship experiences with our lives unchanged and our deepest needs unmet. The apex of worship is when we experience God in a life-changing way. Worship is all about change. When we come together to meet God we are coming for the purpose of becoming more like God. You cannot become more like God without changing. The closer we come to God and each other in worship the more we can expect to experience the blessings of worship.

The key word is "intimacy." Intimacy is the idea of closeness and oneness on an emotional level. We were designed by God to have intimacy (closeness) with Him and each other. It is not easy crossing the gulf of our fear of intimacy and really making a significant connection with the people we see every day. Often it is assumed that if you live with someone, relational intimacy and communication come naturally, but this is not so. Building families that know how to meet each other's needs spiritually and emotionally takes intentional effort. Family worship provides the opportunity for the individual and the group to have their spiritual and relational needs met simultaneously through the power of the Holy Spirit.

Our family included my two sisters, two brothers, my parents and me. It also included on many occasions some non-family members who needed housing and much more. Family worship was the glue to our unique experiences. On one such occasion, while my mother was working for the local housing authority, she invited a 12-year-old, troubled youth from a severely broken family over to our house one night for family worship. Well the short story is, after seeing the love, experiencing the fun (also enjoying the food and being impacted by the Spirit of God through our family worships. He ended up staying and becoming a permanent member of the family for the rest of his life. Presently, he is a committed Christian and minister of the gospel because of the powerful witness from a dynamic family worship experience. One of my sisters requested that she be "conferenced" in by phone for Friday night worships after she moved away. I have countless stories like this of people who would come through our home whose lives are now changed because of the simple, yet profound power of family worship.

Chapter 2
THE PURPOSE

Simply going through the motions of having family worship is not the goal of this book. We want families to experience family worship in such powerful ways that it becomes the most anticipated time of the day. To this point Ellen White said, "In many cases the morning and evening worship is little more than a mere form, a dull, monotonous repetition of set phrases in which the spirit of gratitude or the sense of need finds no expression. The Lord accepts not such service. But the petitions of a humble heart and contrite spirit He will not despise. The opening of our hearts to our heavenly Father, the acknowledgment of our entire dependence, the expression of our wants, the homage of grateful love -- this is true prayer." [5] {CG 518.3} Family worship should be powerful and exciting not monotonous and dull. We also want to help families communicate with each other. Family worship provides a non-threatening therapeutic environment for family members to talk not only about God and spiritual things, but also to help stimulate discussion about family members' needs, hopes and dreams.

Chapter 3
THE PROBLEM

What's wrong with the church? I keep hearing this question everywhere I go. There seems to be a growing frustration with the state of the church. Many are asking this question and everyone seems to have an opinion on the church's current state. There are a myriad of viewpoints but I think we can all agree that the modern church seems to be struggling with living up to its potential. The church is no longer the sleeping giant that needs to be awakened, it seems more accurate to say the church is a dead giant that needs resurrected. We are in many ways grossly underachieving in terms of accomplishing our mission to make disciples. Many of our churches are empty. Our worship services have given way to formalism and routine. It seems to be powerless in its impact on congregants and communities. Marriages and families are falling apart left and right. Fathers have abdicated their God-given responsibility as spiritual leaders and teachers. Mothers are frustrated and struggling to raise Godly children by themselves. Youth are leaving the church in droves. Many are just showing up and going home. Where is the power? Where are the souls being delivered from sin and Satan? We have kept our customs and traditions but lost our families. What is the problem and how do we stop the bleeding? Metaphorically, if the church were a football team, we would be losing the most important game of the season with little time left on the clock. We need solutions and we need them fast.

Some say new or old programs are needed, but programs aren't working. Some say, we preachers need to preach the word. But sermonizing won't change this problem very much either. Others will say we need revival and reformation...the baptism of the Spirit! I agree but where and when should that take place? It seems that we are fighting a war with bows and arrows while the enemy is using nuclear weapons.

What do we do? I would suggest that we need to seek for revival and reformation first in the home and then we will see it spread to the church. The problem with the church has a lot to do with our misconceptions of what the church is. Nowhere in Scripture do we see the church defined as a building or a worship service at a building. The Bible always views the church as a people. The problem with the notion that church is "somewhere you go or something you do" versus "a people" is that it causes us to keep the experience of church at the church and out of our homes!

Our spiritual experience with God should not lose steam or fervor when we leave the church building. As a matter of fact our spiritual experience with God should be as special or better in our homes! We can see the root of this problem by looking at the fruit. Our children (the fruit) reveal the story of what's wrong with our church. What is wrong with our church is that there is plenty wrong in our families (the root or foundation). Our children will show us that our problem is not the church programs or lack thereof. Our children reveal that they are straying from God at home and not at church. The home and the church have reversed roles of spiritual responsibility and have worked separately for the salvation of families, neglecting opportunities

Chapter THREE: The Problem

to work together. In our modern paradigm, the church tries to provide support to the family. The biblical model promotes the opposite. In other words, the idea of church in the Bible extends beyond the walls of a building and institution into our homes. We need to start treating home like church because it is.

The Bible places spiritual responsibility on parents to teach their children the way of the Lord. The basic problem is that families don't view themselves as primarily responsible for spiritual development or even at all. The church should not play the role God gave to the family. The family has bought into the lie that they are supposed to outsource their responsibility to the church. The family must realize that they too are the church and move into their spiritual roles with power and commitment that will cause the enemy of our souls to take flight from our midst.

Chapter 4
TWO POWERFUL CONCEPTS

I can't think of two more powerful concepts than FAMILY and WORSHIP. At creation these were the two foundational principles that God built the human race upon. Adam and Eve representing family and the blessing of the Sabbath representing worship. Both of these ideas originated in the mind of God for the purpose of us knowing and experiencing the power of divine love. In the creation of the first family, God said, "Let us make man in our image, in our likeness…" [6] What an awesome concept! We were made in the image of God! The image of God is not just about His appearance, but more with His character, and His character can be summed up in one word—love. We were created in the image of divine love. The love of God is what gives our lives meaning and purpose. Life without love is meaningless and painful, but when the powerful love of God is experienced in our lives, it gives us a sense of purpose and meaning. Families were designed by God to experience His love, which makes the idea of family so powerful.

Worship is our response to the love of God. Worship does not bring God down on our finite level; rather it brings us up to His level. It calls us to reflect on the worth of God and keeps us focused on his love for us and His great plan for our lives.[7]

When the first family sinned in the Garden of Eden one of the first things they did was hide from the presence of God and avoided worship.[8] Without the presence of God worship cannot take place. In this busy world of competing priorities and values many families are loosing sight of what matters most. Spouses are neglecting their marriages. Parents are neglecting their children. Families are neglecting each other. Above all families are neglecting God. Often in the attempt of families to keep up with the rat-race of life one of the first things goes out the proverbial window is the is the worship of God. So as in the first family, we see how sin and Satan enters into the home. Adam and Eve sought to avoid God because of fear and sin and many families today are not spending time or meaningful time in the presence of God. The enemy wants to keep us away from God and it is his desire to forever separate FAMILY and WORSHIP because he knows when FAMILY and WORSHIP come together there is an explosion of God's love that spreads far beyond the home into the world for generations to come.

In a world where family hurt and pain is at an all-time high, God is calling us back to Him as the solution to our family problems. If there was ever a time to come back to God in worship, the time is now. If there was ever a place where worship should happen, it should be in our homes. If Satan can keep families from worship he can keep them from God. If he can keep them from God, he can keep them from love. If he can keep them from love, he can keep them from each other. If he can keep them from each other, he can isolate them and make them vulnerable to his vicious attacks. However, God knows that if families take the time and make the time each day to worship Him through prayer, praise and the word, they will grow closer to Him and inevitably grow closer to each other and neutralize the power of Satan.

Chapter 5
THE SOLUTION-WHEN GOD SHOWS UP

As a pastor I have the opportunity and privilege to talk and counsel many families both in and out of the church. Many of them are looking for solutions to the negative energy in the painful environments in which they live. Family members want peace in their homes from all the dissension, fighting, negative speaking, abusive behavior, and discouragement that is so pervasive in our society. Home should be a place of blessings and retreat from the craziness of the world, but often people are retreating to the world to seek refuge from the home. Many are over-working, over-shopping, over-playing just to avoid being home. Home should be the last place on earth where you don't feel loved or safe. The reality is many of you, as you read this book, are living in hellish situations and you are on the brink of giving up. I'm a living witness that God can change any situation because there is nothing too hard for Him. As a matter of fact, God is attracted to your problem. He is itching to do something about it. But you have to learn how to make Him feel welcome in your home. When the presence of God is welcome in our home it changes the environment. The Bible says in Psalms 16, "In Your presence is fullness of joy; At Your right hand are pleasures forevermore." [9] God's presence drives out the dark clouds surrounding your home and brings in the "fullness of joy." In other words, the presence of God in the midst of your family presents you with the potential of having a house full of joy. When God shows up, His blessing come with Him. Everything you need for your life is in His presence. You need to know that no matter what the condition of your home life, it can change the moment God shows up. All throughout the New Testament, when Jesus showed up, He brought about change resulting in lives lived in the fullness of joy.

Mark 2 records one of my favorite stories of what the presence of Christ can do when He shows up:

A few days later, when Jesus again entered Capernaum, the people heard that he had come home. They gathered in such large numbers that there was no room left, not even outside the door, and he preached the word to them. Some men came, bringing to him a paralyzed man, carried by four of them. Since they could not get him to Jesus because of the crowd, they made an opening in the roof above Jesus by digging through it and then lowered the mat the man was lying on. When Jesus saw their faith, he said to the paralyzed man, "Son, your sins are forgiven." [10]

The main characters are five men on a mission. One man is paralyzed and is being carried by his four faithful friends throughout the city to find Jesus. These men believed that if they could get their friend in the presence of Jesus that he could be healed, that life could be different and that a possibility of change could become a reality. This is essentially the motivating factor for having family worship. It's the desperate desire to get our problem to Jesus with the confident expectation that He is able to do what He said He would do. . When the four friends finally get to the house where Jesus is, they are presented with an obstacle

Chapter FIVE: Two Powerful Concepts

preventing access to Him--people. —I have discovered that the enemy loves using people to discourage us. At time, coworkers, friends, and even family members will stand between you and your blessing. However, instead of giving up and going back, these four friends became creative or rather, they became "creatively destructive." They were so committed to getting in the presence of Jesus, they decided to rip off the roof and create a makeshift elevator to get their friend to Jesus. You just have to love their ingenuity and the fearlessness they demonstrated on behalf of their friend. The Bible says of this same story in Luke 5:17, "And the power of the Lord was with Jesus to heal the sick." [11] Don't you just love that? Where God's presence is, God's power is. This is the lesson you must learn from this story for your life and your home. Where God's presence is, God's power is. When God is absent from your home life, the odds are stacked up against you. But you change those odds almost immediately in your favor when you seek Him and enter into His presence. Where God's presence is, God's power is. Desperately determine to seek His presence in your home.

Chapter 6
DOES GOD FEEL AT HOME?

One of the worst feelings to have in life is the feeling of being unwanted. Especially when you feel that way about people who are closest to you. It can be very stressful to feel like outsiders and strangers where we are supposed to feel loved and accepted. Often we don't realize that we can feel alone and isolated in a room full of people we know and love. I have discovered loneliness has nothing to do with how many people you have around you. Loneliness is personified when more people are around us. People are made to feel welcome, accepted and loved when we pay attention to them. Notice them. Acknowledge their presence. Talk to them. Celebrate them, not just tolerate them.

How does God feel about feeling welcomed in your home? Is he celebrated or just tolerated.? How do we make him feel welcome? Deuteronomy 6:4-9 gives us a strategy:

"Hear, O Israel: The LORD our God, the LORD is one. Love the LORD your God with all your heart and with all your soul and with all your strength. These commandments that I give you today are to be on your hearts. Impress them on your children. Talk about them

when you sit at home and when you walk along the road, when you lie down and when you get up. Tie them as symbols on your hands and bind them on your foreheads. Write them on the doorframes of your houses and on your gates. (NIV)"

Did you catch the three things in the text that makes God feel welcomed? Here they are: (1) Love God with everything you have; (2) Impress and inspire God's love on those in your family and (3) Talk about God all the time. But there is another crucial idea oozing from this text that we can't afford to miss--the spirituality of families is to be determined at home not outsourced to the church. There should be a Christian lifestyle that is modeled in the home that is not separated as "sacred" or "secular." Home life should be non-stop Jesus! God does not want to be put in a box that we only go to when we need him to get us out of trouble. The text says that the topic of God should be discussed all the time. The believer doesn't "go" to church and then come home. The believing family "lives" church by putting God in everything. The starting point for this is reviving family worship in the home. We have to start seeking God as a part of the regular family life. God should not be quarantined to a church building or specific time once a week, but He should be in everything we do starting at home.

Section 2: Building The Framework

Love the Lord your God with all your heart and with all your soul and with all your strength.
These commandments that I give you today are to be on your hearts. Impress them on your children.
Talk about them when you sit at home and when you walk along the road, when you lie down and when you get up.
Tie them as symbols on your hands and bind them on your foreheads.
Write them on the doorframes of your houses and on your gates.
Deuteronomy 6:5-9 NIV

Chapter 7
WHAT IS FAMILY WORSHIP?

Family worship is when members in a household take time together each day to worship God in specific ways like prayer, praise, and Bible Study. Family worship is a way of inviting the presence of God into the home life by bringing the "church" experience to our homes. The idea of spending time with God is all throughout Scripture, but many times we only see this as a responsibility of individual Christians and churches rather than households and families. The first worship service recorded in the Bible was a family worship with Adam, Eve, and God. And all throughout the Old Testament we see Abraham, Isaac, and Jacob setting up altars throughout their sojourn as places where their families met God in worship. In the New Testament, the early church spent most of their worship time not in the synagogue buildings, but in their homes.[12] The idea of families spending time in the home with God is very much a biblical concept. The only thing needed for family worship to happen is two or more people gathered together with a desire to seek God and strengthen each other.

FOR YOUR STUDY

Biblical References for Family Worship:
- Noah and the family altar (Gen. 8:2)
- Job, the family priest (Job 1:4,5)
- Abraham (Gen. 17:23-27; 18:19)
- Heads of Households in Israel (Deut. 4:9-10; 6:4-9; 11:19-21; 32:46; Ps. 78:1-8)
- Telling the next Generation about God's goodness (Psalm 78)
- Joshua "as for me and my house" (Josh. 24:14-15)
- David and Solomon (2 Sam. 6:20; Prov. 4:1-5)
- House worship (Acts 2:41-47; Acts 5:42)
- Fathers to Children (Eph. 6:4)
- Husbands (1 Pet. 3:7)

Chapter 8
GETTING STARTED: My Attitude

In order to conduct Life-Changing Family Worship, we must first start with having the right attitude and approach. The Bible teaches us that our behavior is influenced by our thinking. Proverbs 23:7 says, "As a man thinks in his heart so is he." [13] The way we think determines how we behave. So it is with family worship, we must have a "life-changing mindset" in order to have a "life-changing family worship."

Three Must-Have Attitudes and Approaches to a Life-Changing Family Worship:
(1) Acceptance
(2) Authenticity
(3) Accountability

1. Acceptance
One of the key characteristics about the love of Christ is that He accepts us unconditionally no matter where we are on our

spiritual journey. To this point, Jesus said, "All those the Father gives me will come to me, and whoever comes to me I will never drive away." [14] When family members engage in family worship, they are coming to the feet of Jesus. Each family member brings whatever baggage they have to Jesus. No matter what we bring, He will accept us because He is a God of unconditional love. Family worship is for family members who are sinners with flaws, wounds, issues, pains, and struggles. The family worship that changes lives must first embrace an attitude of acceptance. When the family enters to worship, there is no family member who is considered as more spiritual than the others. Any mindset of self-righteousness that causes the family to look down on any other family member will stifle the moving of God's spirit. We all recognize our need of God in our lives and when we come together to worship God, we accept each other without prejudice towards any member's situation, circumstance, or personality. God's love, grace, and mercy must guide our conduct when we worship.

2. Authenticity

In order for a deep intimacy and connection with God and each other, family members must be transparent. Although family worship is not primarily a time to deal with all the family problems, it should embrace an attitude that allows people to be themselves and be honest about what's going on in their lives as well as "speak the truth in love." [15] This spirit of authenticity and transparency should be used carefully and with prudence. The Bible teaches there is a "time for everything," but overall, family worship should be an environment where family members can feel comfortable with expressing their feelings without feeling oppressed and suppressed. For example, when family members are praying, their prayers should be open and honest. I remember when my mother knew of a particular struggle concerning one of my family members and she prayed with openness and honesty for God to deliver that family member from a besetting sin. Often times we will ignore the proverbial "elephant in the room" that everyone knows about but no one is talking about. Do not be afraid to pray openly to God about these matters with specificity without endangering or hurting the people involved.

3. Accountability

Accountability is holding people responsible to the will of God in their lives. Family worship should challenge us to become what God wants us to be and to accomplish what God has called us to accomplish. Jesus was constantly holding the disciples accountable to do what he called them to do, so we too should not be afraid to challenge one another to soar beyond our fears and foibles to do "exceedingly, abundantly, above and beyond all that we ask or think." [16]

{ 26 }

Chapter 9
GETTING STARTED: The Components

Worship

Life-Changing Family Worship gatherings should have 5 main components:

(1) Praise

(2) Prayer

(3) Bible Study

(4) Sharing

(5) Encouragement

Praise

Ephesians 5:19, 20 says, "Speaking to one another with psalms, hymns, and songs from the Spirit. Sing and make music from your heart to the Lord, always giving thanks to God the Father for everything, in the name of our Lord Jesus Christ." [17] Praise gives each family member an opportunity to make God big. Praise is the act of speaking or singing about the goodness of God.

It exalts God and helps us to become grateful and count our blessings. Praise refocuses our thoughts away from the power of our problems and redirects us on the power of our God. Praise reminds us of what God has done so that we can be confident of what He will do.

How do you Praise?
The scripture says, I will bless the Lord at all times; His praise shall continually be in my mouth." [18] You praise by talking, testifying, sharing and singing about the goodness of God. Praise helps us to focus on what God has done and who He is. Praise makes God big and your problems small. Praise is a decision. It is not based on your circumstances, but its based on your commitment to stay grateful and positive about what God is doing in your life. Every family worship should always begin with praise and end with praise.

Prayer

Ephesians 6:18 says, "And pray in the Spirit on all occasions with all kinds of prayers and requests. With this in mind, be alert and always keep on praying for all God's people." [19] Prayer is communicating with God. Prayer allows us to gain direct access to where God is and it gives us an opportunity to make requests to God for our needs and desires. Ellen White gives a powerful picture of this idea saying, "If ever there was a time when every house should be a house of prayer, it is now. Infidelity and skepticism prevail. Iniquity abounds. Corruption flows in the vital currents of the soul, and rebellion against God breaks out in the life. Enslaved by sin, the moral powers are under the tyranny of Satan. The soul is made the sport of his temptations; and unless some mighty arm is stretched out to rescue him, man goes where the arch rebel leads the way. And yet, in this time of fearful peril, some who profess to be Christians have no family worship. They do not honor God in the home; they do not teach their children to love and fear Him. Many have separated themselves so far from Him that they feel under condemnation in approaching Him. They cannot 'come boldly unto the throne of grace…lifting up holy hands, without wrath and doubting.' Hebrews 4:16; 1 Timothy 2:8. They have not a living connection with God. Theirs is a form of godliness without the power." [20] As the old adage goes, "Much prayer much power. Little prayer little power. No prayer, no power." God has promised when we call to Him as a family in prayer we put ourselves in a position to expect great things from Him. I love what the Bible says in Jeremiah chapter 33: "Call to me and I will answer you and tell you great and unsearchable things you do not know." [21]

How do you pray?
Families pray by each one talking to God on behalf of each other. Whether they are adults or children, each one can talk to God and no matter the age they can expect God to do great things in answer to their prayer. Family members need to understand that prayer is simply communicating with God. There should be no pressure put on family members to use lofty language in praying or suggesting that there are "good" prayers and "bad" prayers. Prayer should be honest and real. God already know your thoughts so why should we teach people to express anything contrary to what God already knows. Teach your family members to pray with sincerity and authenticity. The bottom line is prayer should be real.

Bible Study

The study of the Scriptures puts the family in a position of hearing the God's word. It is more than information, it is revelation. Information is about facts and principles. Revelation, the noun, not the Bible book, takes facts and principles and applies them to the current situation of the family. Psalm 119:105 says, "Your word is a lamp for my feet, a light on my path." [22] The study of the Scriptures allows us to hear from God so that we might know what to do. Scripture gives direction. When families get into the Word it strengthens their faith in God and His promises, "So then faith comes by hearing, and hearing by the word of God." [23] Faith is one of the greatest needs of families because it is what we need to please God, Hebrews says, "And without faith it is impossible to please God, because anyone who comes to him must believe that he exists and that he rewards those who earnestly seek him." [24] If families are going to build their faith in God they have to build on the solid foundation of bible study.

How to Study the Bible?

Families can study the Bible by reading and discussing the meaning of the scriptures, by studying Bible Devotionals, Bible Storybooks, or any other tool that focuses on the truth of the Bible. Whenever there is a biblical passage read or devotional material, the question should be asked to the individual family members, "What is God saying to you about this?" Personal application of the scriptures is crucial to everyone in the family worship experiencing life change.

▶ Chapter NINE Getting Started: The Components

Sharing

Revelation 12:11 proclaims, "They triumphed over him by the blood of the Lamb and by the word of their testimony...." [25] The meaning of the phrase "the word of their testimony" is the idea of talking about our story (testimony) with one another. When we share with each other our experience with authenticity and transparency it helps us to overcome. Paul supports this idea in 2 Corinthians 1 (verse 2) saying, "Praise be to the God and Father of our Lord Jesus Christ, the Father of compassion and the God of all comfort, who comforts us in all our troubles, so that we can comfort those in any trouble with the comfort we ourselves receive from God." [26] Families bring comfort and strength to each other when they share with each other what's on their hearts and what God has done for them.

How do we share?
Sharing in family worship is simply talking to each other about what God is saying to us or doing inside us. Sharing is also responding to what the God's word means to us. Sharing also gives us an opportunity to talk to our family about our fears, hurts, pains, and even joys.

Encouragement

Intentional effort should be made during family worship to inspire and encourage one another in the faith. Family members, no matter what, should leave the family worship with a general feeling of hope and expectation. Words of affirmation and kindness should be spoken. Spirits should be lifted and positive reinforcement should undergird the worship service. Family members often find themselves in tough situations and negative circumstances; feelings of disappointment and discouragement are a part of everyday life. With this in mind make a concerted effort to speak a word of encouragement in the lives of those present. Our words have the power to build up or destroy. Proverbs says, "The tongue has the power of life and death." [27] Ephesians 4 says, "Do not let any unwholesome talk come out of your mouths, but only what is helpful for building others up according to their needs, that it may benefit those who listen." [28] When God's presence is in our home and in our hearts we will be a blessing to one another with our words, "The mouth of the righteous is a fountain of life." [29] Never leave your time in family worship without speaking a word to one another that will encourage.

How do we encourage?
We encourage by taking time to speak words of affirmation and support throughout the family worship time to each individual who is present. Reminding them that no matter what the situation or the circumstance they "can do all things through Christ," [30] and He will strengthen me. Families should not leave worship without a word of encouragement to them specifically. This can be as simple as saying "You can do this," "God will see you through," or "Don't give up…I have your back."

Chapter 10
7 BENEFITS

Have you noticed that pharmaceutical companies seem to be taking over television commercials these days? I was watching the Super Bowl some years back and noticed that the majority of the ads were about drugs. What's amazing about these commercials is that they are mandated by law to tell you not only the benefits of the drug but also all of the possible side-effects. The crazy thing is that in most of these commercials the side-effects always outnumber the benefits. You would think that after hearing about all the side-effects that people would not buy the drugs, but that is not the case. They are so fixated on the benefits that they trump the side-effects. In the case of Life-Changing Family Worship, I can't think of any negative side-effects, only benefits. The benefits far outweigh the work it takes to keep the flame of family worship burning. Here are seven benefits of Life-Changing family worship.

1. **Spiritual growth** - Families that are intentional about connecting with God and each other when they come together for worship can expect to grow closer to God.

2. **Family Closeness** - Families that are intentional about connecting with God and each other when they come together for worship can expect to grow closer to each other.

3. **Healing** - Families that are intentional about connecting with God and each other can expect to see God bring healing and restoration to broken and wounded situations.

4. **Fun** - Families that are intentional about connecting with God and each other will inevitably have a lot more fun with each other. There is nothing wrong with a little laughter and joy in a Christian home. Proverbs 17:22 says, "A cheerful heart is good medicine, but a crushed spirit dries up the bones."

5. **Educational** - Families that are intentional about connecting with God and each other learn from each other. Families will learn about God, each other and how to lead worship. It also helps to model to children how to pray, study the Bible, praise God, and do His will.

6. **Evangelizing** - Families that are intentional about connecting with God and each other will find that it creates a great opportunity and venue to invite people who need God to experience it in a non-threatening environment. People are more likely to come to your home than come to your church.

▶ Chapter TEN: 7 Benefits

7. **Family Health** - No matter how dysfunctional your family is, when families spend time in the presence of God together on a regular basis, this will help promote a strong family well-being and morale. The more families spend time together with God the more emotionally, relationally and spiritually healthy they will be.

Chapter 11
THE TEN COMMANDMENTS OF FAMILY WORSHIP

1. **Thou shalt set a time** - A time should be set that can involve all family members. It is preferable to have family worship twice a day; in the morning and the evening. However some families have different schedule circumstances and will need to select a time that works best for them. But remember, you must make time not just set a time to spend in family worship. Make a commitment as a family that you will not go one day without spending some time with God together!

2. **Thou shalt be consistent** - Consistency does not mean that you never miss a day; it just means "come what may" you keep at it and don't give up. You will not be perfect at this, but be committed and faithful to the process.

3. **Thou shalt minimize distractions** - Avoid doing family worship while multi-tasking. Such as watching TV, using the computer or conducting any other competing activities. Keep the focus on God and each other. It is also helpful to select a space that is conducive for worship.

4. **Remember the Sabbath family worship to make it special** - When the sun sets on Friday make sure that you have planned for a special family worship that is different from the others. When the sun sets on Saturday evening gather your family together to thank God for the blessings of the Sabbath day experience. You can also give family members the opportunity to discuss the blessings experienced during the hours of the Sabbath.

5. **Parents shall be responsible for leading and planning worship** - The father/husband is the priest of the home and responsible for facilitating family worship and biblical instruction. This does not mean that he always has to lead out; it simply means that he is responsible for it happening and happening in a life-changing way. He will often delegate responsibilities to others in the family but he is the driving force behind family worship. In homes where there is no Father/Husband, whoever is the leader of the household should be responsible for the family worship (i.e. single parent homes, singles, etc.)

6. **Thou shalt not be boring** - Family worship should be exciting, intriguing and attractive to those in the home.

Chapter ELEVEN: The Ten Commandments

It should not be a monotonous rehearsal of rituals, but an exciting experience with God and others. In order for this to happen, planning and thought must go into the family worship time before it happens.

7. **Thou shalt not be long** - Keep the family worship brief and concise if at all possible. I would suggest no longer than 10-20 minutes.

8. **Thou shalt cater to the youth** - If you have any youth in your home the songs selected, Scriptures used and the way worship is carried out should be catered to the youth primarily. If you focus on the youth everyone will be blessed. If you focus only on adults you run the risk of alienating the youth.

9. **Everyone shalt participate** - One person should not dominate the family worship. Everyone should be given a part to play in every component of the worship. This engenders participation and interest in the family worship.

10. **Thou shalt invite others to come to your family worship** - When it is possible invite others outside of your family and even your church to come to your family worship. Remember family worship can be a most effective evangelistic tool in reaching others. From time to time especially on Friday night invite friends, family and non-church members to join you for your family worship with a special meal prepared.

Chapter 12
WHERE & WHEN

Where Should we Have Family Worship?

It is important that Family worship happens in the right setting. Location is not as important as environment. You can have family worship wherever there will be minimal competing distractions for your family's time in God's presence. It is especially important to make sure that wherever you are in your home, in the car, even outdoors that you don't allow kids to play with toys, things like reading books or magazines that have nothing to do with the worship, or working on the computer, or watching TV. The key to location is focus. All should be exclusively focused on and engaged in the family worship.

When Should we Have Family Worship?

In our busy culture today it becomes increasingly difficult to find time for important things, especially spiritual things. Satan doesn't care if we are doing so called "bad" things, he just wants to make our lives are so busy that we don't make time or have time for 'good things. We have to literally fight to have time with God. Family worship will not happen naturally in the flow of our hectic lives, it must be planned and scheduled. So, when should we schedule family worship? I would suggest that family worship should be treated like bookends. If at all possible, considering that every family has a different schedule, family worship should be at the beginning of the day and the end of the day. The idea is that you need to start your day right seeking God and end the day right by debriefing with God. When worship happens more than once a day in the home it is a constant reminder to the family that this home is a holy place where God lives. Never let anything get in the way of this most sacred time with God. We should be as committed to family worship during the week as we are to attending church on the weekend.

Chapter 13
THE POWER OF 40

It is said that it takes 21 days to break a habit or establish one. I have witnessed this reality in my own life. In order for us to completely solidify family worship as natural habit of family life, we believe that we should almost double the 21- day rule of habit formation. After 40 days of repeating a behavior it will become more than habit, it will become a lifestyle. The idea of 40 also has significant strong Biblical significance. Forty is seen as the number of preparation for major changes and transformations. It rained 40 days and 40 nights as Noah and his family were tucked safely in the ark waiting for God to cleanse sin-cursed earth with the flood. Moses was on Mt. Sinai with God for 40 days receiving His laws and commands for the Israelites. Before David slew the giant Goliath with a sling and stone it was preceded by 40 days and 40 nights of Goliath taunting the armies of Israel. Jesus fasted and prayed for 40 days and 40 nights before He started His powerful earthly ministry. When you see 40 days in the Bible you come to expect and prepare for a divine visitation of God's transformative power. This spiritual time frame is the spiritual boot-camp for the manifestation of God's purpose and blessings in your life.

I have designed a 40-day challenge that can be used to help foster more meaningful family worships. The reason I call them challenges is because they will not be easy or feel normal. They are specifically designed to jumpstart a revival in your family that you stand in need of. They will strengthen your family's spirituality and unity. If they are followed faithfully, your family will not be the same. It takes work and commitment but as the old saying goes, "if you aim at nothing you will hit it every time." These 40 days of challenges are intentional attempts to aim at total transformation and life change in your family and if you follow these with a sincere heart for revival you will hit your target. The challenges are designed to be used with, and during your family worship time. The 40 challenges are divided into six sections for the six weeks you will do this. These are not to dominate the family worship but to enhance the family worship time. The 40- day challenge works best when it starts on a Sunday through Saturday seven-day week cycle. Are you ready to take the challenge?

Chapter 14
FOR MAXIMUM RESULTS

There are some families searching for a major blessing in their home life. They are past desperate. They are at the point of a spiritual emergency and they need God to move in a profound way. For maximum results in any spiritual venture, the Bible always combines prayer and fasting. In Mark 9, there is a story recorded of a father with a major family crisis. His son was being tormented by a demon that had robbed him of his ability to speak. I like the example this father sets because he demonstrates to us what a family leader should do when he or she recognizes the attack of the enemy on the family. He brings his son to Jesus. Jesus heals the boy of his demonic torment and sets him free, bringing peace and joy back to this family. Before Jesus came to the rescue of this family, the disciples had unsuccessfully tried to cast the devil out of the boy. Blown away by the authority that Jesus demonstrated over the evil spirit, the crestfallen and humiliated disciples pulled Jesus aside privately and asked Him "Why couldn't we drive it out?" Jesus response gives us the answer on how to get maximum results out of this 40-day challenge when he said, "This kind can come out by nothing but prayer and fasting (verse 29). I hope you didn't miss that. The disciples were good church-going followers of Christ but were unable to deal with the devil in this man's family. Jesus exposes the reason for their failure--they were not connected to God. Practically speaking, Jesus suggests that prayer, worship, and the like is made more powerful when it is accompanied by fasting. Prayer and fasting is double trouble for the devil and his kingdom. If you want to get the most out of the 40-day Life Changing Family Worship Challenge then I suggest to you to combine the next 40 days with a family-friendly fast which I will outline below.

What is Family Friendly Fast?
Biblical fasting is generally when you deny yourself food or drink for a period of time for the purpose of seeking God. It is an act of self-denial and sacrifice that says, "I want God so bad that I am willing to deny my secondary (food, drink, T.V., Facebook, etc.) needs for my primary need (God).

A Family Friendly Fast takes into consideration the different levels of spiritual commitment and growth of each family member and selects mutually agreed pleasures to forsake for this 40-day time period.

Recommended Family Friendly Fast for the 40-day Life-Changing Family Worship Challenge.

No Secular Media!
Is that it? Yup! But that's really a lot. Actually that is a major sacrifice for most of us. The average American Family spends 4-5 hours watching TV a day. That doesn't include other secular media, like the Internet which includes addictive social media

Chapter FOURTEEN: For Maximum Results

outlets like Facebook and Twitter. For 40 days, we suggest that you fast from T.V. and social media. I know you are asking, "What are we supposed to do with our time when there is no T.V. and social media?" I suggest that you actually spend time together! Play games together. Work on family projects together. Go visit someone. Finish that to-do list of chores. Go on a family outing. Spend time in the Word. The point is, be productive. Watching T.V. and spending hours on social media is counter-productive to the spiritual growth process you desire for your family to experience. You can do this. You can make it 40 days without secular media in order to get your blessing. I promise you what you will be giving up cannot compare to what you will gain from God.

{ 48 }

One well-ordered, well-disciplined family tells more in behalf of Christianity than all the sermons that can be preached.
The Adventist Home, by Ellen White

{ 50 }

Week 1

"FEELING GOOD"
Family Closeness

Dear friends, let us continue to love one another, for love comes from God. Anyone who loves is a child of God and knows God.

1 John 4:7 NLT

Day 1 "10 Seconds of Love"

> **LIFE-CHANGING FAMILY WORSHIP FORMAT**
>
> SING • Sing a song(s) of praise that everyone can enjoy.
> PRAY • Pray for God's presence to fill every heart.
> BIBLE • Read short and brief text (Life-Changing Idea and Life-Changing Scripture) or a story from the Bible.
> SHARE • Have everyone share what they've learned as well as prayer requests and praise reports.

Life-Changing Scripture: Dear friends, let us continue to love one another, for love comes from God. Anyone who loves is a child of God and knows God. 1 John 4:7 NLT

Life-Changing Idea: Hugs reduce stress. Families should give a lot of hugs each day as a means of reducing household stress. Never leave each other's presence for extended periods of time without a hug.

Life-Changing Challenge: Everyone should hug each family member. The hug should last for 10 seconds.

Day 2 "10 Seconds of Love The Sequel"

>> **LIFE - CHANGING FAMILY WORSHIP FORMAT**

SING	• Sing a song(s) of praise that everyone can enjoy.
PRAY	• Pray for God's presence to fill every heart.
BIBLE	• Read short and brief text (Life-Changing Idea and Life-Changing Scripture) or a story from the Bible.
SHARE	• Have everyone share what they've learned as well as prayer requests and praise reports.

Life-Changing Scripture: Dear friends, let us continue to love one another, for love comes from God. Anyone who loves is a child of God and knows God. 1 John 4:7 NLT

Life-Changing Idea: A great way to experience God's love is by giving away the love that you have received from Him.

Life-Changing Challenge: At the end of worship each family member will give a hug to each family member. The hug should last for 10 seconds and then look them in their eye and say, "I love you very much."

Day 3 "A Hug and a Prayer"

> **LIFE - CHANGING FAMILY WORSHIP FORMAT**
>
> **SING** • Sing a song(s) of praise that everyone can enjoy.
> **PRAY** • Pray for God's presence to fill every heart.
> **BIBLE** • Read short and brief text (Life-Changing Idea and Life-Changing Scripture) or a story from the Bible.
> **SHARE** • Have everyone share what they've learned as well as prayer requests and praise reports.

Life-Changing Scripture: Dear friends, let us continue to love one another, for love comes from God. Anyone who loves is a child of God and knows God. 1 John 4:7 NLT

Life-Changing Idea: God gives us the ability to bless Him and others, be a blessing and don't just expect a blessing.

Life-Changing Challenge: At the end of worship each family member will give a hug to each family member. The hug should last for 10 seconds and then look them in their eye and say, "I love you very much" and then while embraced take turns offering a prayer of blessing for the other.

Day 4 "Group Hug Prayer"

> **LIFE - CHANGING FAMILY WORSHIP FORMAT**
>
> SING • Sing a song(s) of praise that everyone can enjoy.
> PRAY • Pray for God's presence to fill every heart.
> BIBLE • Read short and brief text (Life-Changing Idea and Life-Changing Scripture) or a story from the Bible.
> SHARE • Have everyone share what they've learned as well as prayer requests and praise reports.

Life-Changing Scripture: Dear friends, let us continue to love one another, for love comes from God. Anyone who loves is a child of God and knows God. 1 John 4:7 NLT

Life-Changing Idea: It drives Satan crazy to see families who love each other. Drive him crazy today.

Life-Changing Challenge: At the end of family worship all the family members will form a group hug by placing their arms around each family member's shoulders in a circle. Once the group hug has been formed, each family member will say a sentence prayer for the family.

Day 5 "I love you because"

> **LIFE-CHANGING FAMILY WORSHIP FORMAT**
>
> **SING** • Sing a song(s) of praise that everyone can enjoy.
> **PRAY** • Pray for God's presence to fill every heart.
> **BIBLE** • Read short and brief text (Life-Changing Idea and Life-Changing Scripture) or a story from the Bible.
> **SHARE** • Have everyone share what they've learned as well as prayer requests and praise reports.

Life-Changing Scripture: Dear friends, let us continue to love one another, for love comes from God. Anyone who loves is a child of God and knows God. 1 John 4:7 NLT

Life-Changing Idea: Actions speaks louder than words, but never underestimate the power of saying and hearing a sincere, "I love you." Love must not only be demonstrated it must be said.

Life-Changing Challenge: During the family worship, each family member should tell the other family members why they love them so much.

Day 6 "Let's Eat! Together."

> **LIFE - CHANGING FAMILY WORSHIP FORMAT**
>
> SING • Sing a song(s) of praise that everyone can enjoy.
> PRAY • Pray for God's presence to fill every heart.
> BIBLE • Read short and brief text (Life-Changing Idea and Life-Changing Scripture) or a story from the Bible.
> SHARE • Have everyone share what they've learned as well as prayer requests and praise reports.

Life-Changing Scripture: Dear friends, let us continue to love one another, for love comes from God. Anyone who loves is a child of God and knows God. 1 John 4:7 NLT

Life-Changing Idea: Make up your mind that you will be intentional about making every family member feel special.

Life-Changing Challenge: Plan to share a meal together at home this evening as a family after worship.

Day 7 "I thank God for you because…"

> **LIFE - CHANGING FAMILY WORSHIP FORMAT**
>
> SING • Sing a song(s) of praise that everyone can enjoy.
> PRAY • Pray for God's presence to fill every heart.
> BIBLE • Read short and brief text (Life-Changing Idea and Life-Changing Scripture) or a story from the Bible.
> SHARE • Have everyone share what they've learned as well as prayer requests and praise reports.

Life-Changing Scripture: Dear friends, let us continue to love one another, for love comes from God. Anyone who loves is a child of God and knows God. 1 John 4:7 NLT

Life-Changing Idea: There is life and death in the power of the tongue (Proverbs 18:21). Use your words today to speak life to your family members. Today God wants to speak to someone in your family words of encouragement. Let Him use your mouth.

Life-Changing Challenge: At some point during family worship, each family member should pick one family member and tell them one reason why you thank God for them this week. For example, "I would like to thank God for my mother this week because she has really made an effort to see how I am doing."

Week 2

"WORDS MATTER"
Words of Affirmation

Don't use foul or abusive language.
Let everything you say be good and helpful,
so that your words will be an encouragement to those who hear them.

Ephesians 4:29 NLT

Day 8 "Words of Affirmation - Parents"

> **LIFE - CHANGING FAMILY WORSHIP FORMAT**
>
> **SING** • Sing a song(s) of praise that everyone can enjoy.
> **PRAY** • Pray for God's presence to fill every heart.
> **BIBLE** • Read short and brief text (Life-Changing Idea and Life-Changing Scripture) or a story from the Bible.
> **SHARE** • Have everyone share what they've learned as well as prayer requests and praise reports.

Life-Changing Scripture: Don't use foul or abusive language. Let everything you say be good and helpful, so that your words will be an encouragement to those who hear them. Ephesians 4:29 NLT

Life-Changing Idea: It takes less time and effort to demolish a building instead of constructing one. So it is with encouraging people. Our tendency is to complain and tear down. Make the extra effort to build up members of your family with words of encouragement today.

Life-Changing Challenge: During the family worship the parents of the household should affirm the children with positive words, such as, "Justin, I want to affirm you for keeping the house clean, it means a lot."

Day 9 "Words of Affirmation - Kids"

» LIFE - CHANGING FAMILY WORSHIP FORMAT

SING	• Sing a song(s) of praise that everyone can enjoy.
PRAY	• Pray for God's presence to fill every heart.
BIBLE	• Read short and brief text (Life-Changing Idea and Life-Changing Scripture) or a story from the Bible.
SHARE	• Have everyone share what they've learned as well as prayer requests and praise reports.

Life-Changing Scripture: Don't use foul or abusive language. Let everything you say be good and helpful, so that your words will be an encouragement to those who hear them. Ephesians 4:29 NLT

Life-Changing Idea: Words can produce life. A dead house usually ends up that way because of the kinds of words spoken. A house that is alive with love is a house where words of affirmation are free flowing like the air we breathe. Produce some verbal oxygen in your home today.

Life-Changing Challenge: During the family worship the kids will affirm the parents (adults) by stating what they appreciate about them, for example "Dad, I really appreciate the sacrifices you make for us by working so hard. Thank you so much for all you do."

Day 10 "I just called to say I love you"

> **LIFE-CHANGING FAMILY WORSHIP FORMAT**
>
> SING • Sing a song(s) of praise that everyone can enjoy.
> PRAY • Pray for God's presence to fill every heart.
> BIBLE • Read short and brief text (Life-Changing Idea and Life-Changing Scripture) or a story from the Bible.
> SHARE • Have everyone share what they've learned as well as prayer requests and praise reports.

Life-Changing Scripture: Don't use foul or abusive language. Let everything you say be good and helpful, so that your words will be an encouragement to those who hear them. Ephesians 4:29 NLT

Life-Changing Idea: Don't assume that people know you love them. Tell them.

Life-Changing Challenge: At the end of the family worship, call a family member that is not present and simply tell them, "We just called to say we love you" and then pray for them on the phone.

Day 11 "Speak No Evil"

>> LIFE - CHANGING FAMILY WORSHIP FORMAT

SING	• Sing a song(s) of praise that everyone can enjoy.
PRAY	• Pray for God's presence to fill every heart.
BIBLE	• Read short and brief text (Life-Changing Idea and Life-Changing Scripture) or a story from the Bible.
SHARE	• Have everyone share what they've learned as well as prayer requests and praise reports.

Life-Changing Scripture: Don't use foul or abusive language. Let everything you say be good and helpful, so that your words will be an encouragement to those who hear them. Ephesians 4:29 NLT

Life-Changing Idea: If you don't have anything kind and constructive to say. Keep your mouth shut.

Life-Changing Challenge: For the next 24 hours, attempt to say nothing negative, make no complaints or say anything hurtful to or about any one of your family members.

Day 12 "I thank God for you because..."

>> LIFE-CHANGING FAMILY WORSHIP FORMAT

SING	• Sing a song(s) of praise that everyone can enjoy.
PRAY	• Pray for God's presence to fill every heart.
BIBLE	• Read short and brief text (Life-Changing Idea and Life-Changing Scripture) or a story from the Bible.
SHARE	• Have everyone share what they've learned as well as prayer requests and praise reports.

Life-Changing Scripture: Don't use foul or abusive language. Let everything you say be good and helpful, so that your words will be an encouragement to those who hear them. Ephesians 4:29 NLT

Life-Changing Idea: When we show appreciation we are saying more than "thank you" we are saying people have value.

Life-Changing Challenge: At some point during family worship each family member should pick one family member and tell them one reason why you thank God for them this week. For example, "I would like to thank God for my mother this week because she has really made an effort to see how I am doing."

Day 13 "Let's Eat! Together."

> **LIFE - CHANGING FAMILY WORSHIP FORMAT**
>
> SING • Sing a song(s) of praise that everyone can enjoy.
> PRAY • Pray for God's presence to fill every heart.
> BIBLE • Read short and brief text (Life-Changing Idea and Life-Changing Scripture) or a story from the Bible.
> SHARE • Have everyone share what they've learned as well as prayer requests and praise reports.

Life-Changing Scripture: Don't use foul or abusive language. Let everything you say be good and helpful, so that your words will be an encouragement to those who hear them. Ephesians 4:29 NLT

Life-Changing Idea: Eating together as a family is important. It is a practical way of remembering "we are a unified family"

Life-Changing Challenge: Plan to share a meal together at home this evening as a family after worship.

Day 14 "Family Walk"

▶▶ LIFE - CHANGING FAMILY WORSHIP FORMAT

SING	• Sing a song(s) of praise that everyone can enjoy.
PRAY	• Pray for God's presence to fill every heart.
BIBLE	• Read short and brief text (Life-Changing Idea and Life-Changing Scripture) or a story from the Bible.
SHARE	• Have everyone share what they've learned as well as prayer requests and praise reports.

Life-Changing Scripture: Don't use foul or abusive language. Let everything you say be good and helpful, so that your words will be an encouragement to those who hear them. Ephesians 4:29 NLT

Life-Changing Idea: Families do things together, not apart.

Life-Changing Challenge: At some point today take a walk as a family.

Week 3

"WE NEED HEALING"
Family Healing

*If my people, who are called by my name,
will humble themselves and pray and seek my face and turn from their wicked ways,
then will I hear from heaven and will forgive their sin and will heal their land.*

2 Chronicles 7:14 NIV

Day 15 "Family Prayer Journal"

>> LIFE-CHANGING FAMILY WORSHIP FORMAT

SING	• Sing a song(s) of praise that everyone can enjoy.
PRAY	• Pray for God's presence to fill every heart.
BIBLE	• Read short and brief text (Life-Changing Idea and Life-Changing Scripture) or a story from the Bible.
SHARE	• Have everyone share what they've learned as well as prayer requests and praise reports.

Life-Changing Scripture: If my people, who are called by my name, will humble themselves and pray and seek my face and turn from their wicked ways, then will I hear from heaven and will forgive their sin and will heal their land. 2 Chronicles 7:14 NIV

Life-Changing Idea: Satan is afraid of a family that prays together. Put some fear in his heart.

Life-Changing Challenge: Have someone to purchase a family prayer journal. This journal will be used to write down the family requests for prayer and as the prayers are answered they should be marked "Answered Prayer."

Day 16 "Prayer Requests"

>> **LIFE - CHANGING FAMILY WORSHIP FORMAT**

SING	• Sing a song(s) of praise that everyone can enjoy.
PRAY	• Pray for God's presence to fill every heart.
BIBLE	• Read short and brief text (Life-Changing Idea and Life-Changing Scripture) or a story from the Bible.
SHARE	• Have everyone share what they've learned as well as prayer requests and praise reports.

Life-Changing Scripture: If my people, who are called by my name, will humble themselves and pray and seek my face and turn from their wicked ways, then will I hear from heaven and will forgive their sin and will heal their land.
2 Chronicles 7:14 NIV

Life-Changing Idea: Did you realize that God is waiting on your prayers. Don't keep him waiting.

Life-Changing Challenge: In the family prayer journal, write down family prayer requests as expressed by every member of the family. Then take time to pray over the requests.

Day 17 "Heal Us"

>> **LIFE-CHANGING FAMILY WORSHIP FORMAT**

SING	• Sing a song(s) of praise that everyone can enjoy.
PRAY	• Pray for God's presence to fill every heart.
BIBLE	• Read short and brief text (Life-Changing Idea and Life-Changing Scripture) or a story from the Bible.
SHARE	• Have everyone share what they've learned as well as prayer requests and praise reports.

Life-Changing Scripture: If my people, who are called by my name, will humble themselves and pray and seek my face and turn from their wicked ways, then will I hear from heaven and will forgive their sin and will heal their land. 2 Chronicles 7:14 NIV

Life-Changing Idea: It is an insult to God to settle for dysfunction. Don't settle for anything less than God's best for your life. He desires that you prosper and be in health (3 John 2). Healing is not just for the body, it's for the soul. Seek it until your're made whole.

Life-Changing Challenge: Specifically identify one particular family problem that needs healing from God that all family members agree on. Write it down on a separate page and write a Bible promise on that page claiming God's word to heal this situation.

Day 18 "I need Healing"

> **LIFE-CHANGING FAMILY WORSHIP FORMAT**
>
> SING • Sing a song(s) of praise that everyone can enjoy.
> PRAY • Pray for God's presence to fill every heart.
> BIBLE • Read short and brief text (Life-Changing Idea and Life-Changing Scripture) or a story from the Bible.
> SHARE • Have everyone share what they've learned as well as prayer requests and praise reports.

Life-Changing Scripture: If my people, who are called by my name, will humble themselves and pray and seek my face and turn from their wicked ways, then will I hear from heaven and will forgive their sin and will heal their land. 2 Chronicles 7:14 NIV

Life-Changing Idea: Pray big prayers. Expect God to blow your mind. God wants to do more than you can ask or imagine (Ephesians 3:20). Don't limit him with your fear and lack of faith. He's Able!

Life-Changing Challenge: Each family member should express to the family an individual area that needs God's healing. Children will need help to identifying areas in this challenge. Once expressed, someone will offer prayer for the whole group.

Day 19 "Healing Circle"

> **LIFE - CHANGING FAMILY WORSHIP FORMAT**
>
> | | |
> |---|---|
> | SING | • Sing a song(s) of praise that everyone can enjoy. |
> | PRAY | • Pray for God's presence to fill every heart. |
> | BIBLE | • Read short and brief text (Life-Changing Idea and Life-Changing Scripture) or a story from the Bible. |
> | SHARE | • Have everyone share what they've learned as well as prayer requests and praise reports. |

Life-Changing Scripture: If my people, who are called by my name, will humble themselves and pray and seek my face and turn from their wicked ways, then will I hear from heaven and will forgive their sin and will heal their land. 2 Chronicles 7:14 NIV

Life-Changing Idea: Anyone can pray. The power of prayer is not based on the words or status of the person praying. The power of prayer is based on the sincerity of the heart of the one who prays. Don't be afraid to pray. God is not interested in your words but you.

Life-Changing Challenge: Take the time to place each family member within a prayer circle. Have the family member in the circle to kneel/sit while everyone else stands. Then, each family member will place their hands on the head and shoulders of the family member in the circle. While they are doing this they will pray for healing in that family member's life.

Day 20 "Let's Eat! Together."

> **LIFE - CHANGING FAMILY WORSHIP FORMAT**
>
> | | |
> |---|---|
> | SING | • Sing a song(s) of praise that everyone can enjoy. |
> | PRAY | • Pray for God's presence to fill every heart. |
> | BIBLE | • Read short and brief text (Life-Changing Idea and Life-Changing Scripture) or a story from the Bible. |
> | SHARE | • Have everyone share what they've learned as well as prayer requests and praise reports. |

Life-Changing Scripture: If my people, who are called by my name, will humble themselves and pray and seek my face and turn from their wicked ways, then will I hear from heaven and will forgive their sin and will heal their land.
2 Chronicles 7:14 NIV

Life-Changing Idea: If you love God then the first place it should be seen is in your family.

Life-Changing Challenge: Plan to share a meal together at home this evening as a family after family worship.

Day 21 "We Have the Victory"

> **LIFE-CHANGING FAMILY WORSHIP FORMAT**
>
> SING • Sing a song(s) of praise that everyone can enjoy.
> PRAY • Pray for God's presence to fill every heart.
> BIBLE • Read short and brief text (Life-Changing Idea and Life-Changing Scripture) or a story from the Bible.
> SHARE • Have everyone share what they've learned as well as prayer requests and praise reports.

Life-Changing Scripture: If my people, who are called by my name, will humble themselves and pray and seek my face and turn from their wicked ways, then will I hear from heaven and will forgive their sin and will heal their land. 2 Chronicles 7:14 NIV

Life-Changing Idea: Complaining people are individuals who suffer from "spiritual amnesia." Counting your blessings makes it hard to complain.

Life-Changing Challenge: Review the family journal and see where God has answered prayer requests. Then say a prayer of thanksgiving for what God has done.

Week 4

"WHAT IS OUR FAMILY VISION"
Family Vision

Where there is no vision, the people perish: but he that keeps the law, happy is he.
Proverbs 29:18 KJV

Call unto me, and I will answer thee, and shew thee great and mighty things, which thou knowest not.
Jeremiah 33:3 KJV

Day 22 "Pray for Vision"

> **LIFE - CHANGING FAMILY WORSHIP FORMAT**
>
> | | |
> |---|---|
> | SING | • Sing a song(s) of praise that everyone can enjoy. |
> | PRAY | • Pray for God's presence to fill every heart. |
> | BIBLE | • Read short and brief text (Life-Changing Idea and Life-Changing Scripture) or a story from the Bible. |
> | SHARE | • Have everyone share what they've learned as well as prayer requests and praise reports. |

Life-Changing Scripture: Where there is no vision, the people perish: but he that keeps the law, happy is he. Proverbs 29:18 KJV. Call unto me, and I will answer thee, and shew thee great and mighty things, which thou knowest not. Jeremiah 33:3 KJV

Life-Changing Idea: There is a purpose for your pain and ministry can come from your mess.

Life-Changing Challenge: As a family, spend some time in prayer asking God to reveal a family vision or purpose to the family.

Day 23 "A Healing Call"

> **LIFE - CHANGING FAMILY WORSHIP FORMAT**
>
> SING • Sing a song(s) of praise that everyone can enjoy.
> PRAY • Pray for God's presence to fill every heart.
> BIBLE • Read short and brief text (Life-Changing Idea and Life-Changing Scripture) or a story from the Bible.
> SHARE • Have everyone share what they've learned as well as prayer requests and praise reports.

Life-Changing Scripture: Where there is no vision, the people perish: but he that keeps the law, happy is he. Proverbs 29:18 KJV. Call unto me, and I will answer thee, and shew thee great and mighty things, which thou knowest not. Jeremiah 33:3 KJV

Life-Changing Idea: Don't wait for someone to tell you they need prayer, ask God to show you who to pray for, then call them and pray for them.

Life-Changing Challenge: At the end of family worship, call a family member in need of any kind of healing and pray that God would provide the healing that they need.

Day 24 "Family S.W.O.T Analysis"

►► LIFE - CHANGING FAMILY WORSHIP FORMAT

SING	• Sing a song(s) of praise that everyone can enjoy.
PRAY	• Pray for God's presence to fill every heart.
BIBLE	• Read short and brief text (Life-Changing Idea and Life-Changing Scripture) or a story from the Bible.
SHARE	• Have everyone share what they've learned as well as prayer requests and praise reports.

Life-Changing Scripture: Where there is no vision, the people perish: but he that keeps the law, happy is he. Proverbs 29:18 KJV. Call unto me, and I will answer thee, and shew thee great and mighty things, which thou knowest not. Jeremiah 33:3 KJV

Life-Changing Idea: Spend less time looking at everyone else's flaws and issues and spend more time looking at yours. The more you see God the more you will see yourself. The more you see yourself, the more you will want Jesus.

Life-Changing Challenge: Spend some time in your family prayer journal writing down two of each of the following areas: What are the STRENGTHS, WEAKNESSES, OPPORTUNITIES, AND THREATS concerning our family?

Day 25 "Goal Focused"

> **LIFE-CHANGING FAMILY WORSHIP FORMAT**
>
> SING • Sing a song(s) of praise that everyone can enjoy.
> PRAY • Pray for God's presence to fill every heart.
> BIBLE • Read short and brief text (Life-Changing Idea and Life-Changing Scripture) or a story from the Bible.
> SHARE • Have everyone share what they've learned as well as prayer requests and praise reports.

Life-Changing Scripture: Where there is no vision, the people perish: but he that keeps the law, happy is he. Proverbs 29:18 KJV. Call unto me, and I will answer thee, and shew thee great and mighty things, which thou knowest not. Jeremiah 33:3 KJV

Life-Changing Idea: If you aim at nothing you will hit it every time. Aim at Jesus and you will hit Him every time. Stop day dreaming and Plan. Prepare. Execute.

Life-Changing Challenge: Write down and post where all the family members can see three family goals you want to accomplish going forward. Pray over them.

Day 26 "Praying for the goals"

▶▶ LIFE - CHANGING FAMILY WORSHIP FORMAT

SING	• Sing a song(s) of praise that everyone can enjoy.
PRAY	• Pray for God's presence to fill every heart.
BIBLE	• Read short and brief text (Life-Changing Idea and Life-Changing Scripture) or a story from the Bible.
SHARE	• Have everyone share what they've learned as well as prayer requests and praise reports.

Life-Changing Scripture: Where there is no vision, the people perish: but he that keeps the law, happy is he. Proverbs 29:18 KJV. Call unto me, and I will answer thee, and shew thee great and mighty things, which thou knowest not. Jeremiah 33:3 KJV

Life-Changing Idea: Failure in life often begins when we make our own plans first, and then give them to God. How about asking God what His plans are and then praying for the courage to perform them.

Life-Changing Challenge: Take time today to pray specifically for God to help you accomplish each goal. Name them and claim them in your prayer.

Day 27 "Let's Eat! Together."

> **LIFE-CHANGING FAMILY WORSHIP FORMAT**
>
> | | |
> |---|---|
> | SING | • Sing a song(s) of praise that everyone can enjoy. |
> | PRAY | • Pray for God's presence to fill every heart. |
> | BIBLE | • Read short and brief text (Life-Changing Idea and Life-Changing Scripture) or a story from the Bible. |
> | SHARE | • Have everyone share what they've learned as well as prayer requests and praise reports. |

Life-Changing Scripture: Where there is no vision, the people perish: but he that keeps the law, happy is he. Proverbs 29:18 KJV. Call unto me, and I will answer thee, and shew thee great and mighty things, which thou knowest not. Jeremiah 33:3 KJV

Life-Changing Idea: No matter what your family has gone through God has his Hands on you. He is not afraid of your issues neither is he caught off guard. He has his hands on you. Believe that!

Life-Changing Challenge: Plan to share a meal together at home this evening as a family after family worship.

Day 28 "Praying for Family Weaknesses"

> **LIFE-CHANGING FAMILY WORSHIP FORMAT**
>
> SING • Sing a song(s) of praise that everyone can enjoy.
> PRAY • Pray for God's presence to fill every heart.
> BIBLE • Read short and brief text (Life-Changing Idea and Life-Changing Scripture) or a story from the Bible.
> SHARE • Have everyone share what they've learned as well as prayer requests and praise reports.

Life-Changing Scripture: Where there is no vision, the people perish: but he that keeps the law, happy is he. Proverbs 29:18 KJV. Call unto me, and I will answer thee, and shew thee great and mighty things, which thou knowest not. Jeremiah 33:3 KJV

Life-Changing Idea: God is attracted to weakness.

Life-Changing Challenge: Have each family member to write down one major family weakness and then pray for God to bring help and healing to that weakness.

Week 5

"WE HAVE A MINISTRY"
Family Ministry

"Therefore go and make disciples of all nations..."
Matthew 28:19 NIV

Day 29 "Baptism"

> **LIFE - CHANGING FAMILY WORSHIP FORMAT**
>
> SING • Sing a song(s) of praise that everyone can enjoy.
> PRAY • Pray for God's presence to fill every heart.
> BIBLE • Read short and brief text (Life-Changing Idea and Life-Changing Scripture) or a story from the Bible.
> SHARE • Have everyone share what they've learned as well as prayer requests and praise reports.

Life-Changing Scripture: "Therefore go and make disciples of all nations..." Matthew 28:19 NIV

Life-Changing Idea: Baptism is not graduation its pre-school. Its the beginning of our walk with God not the end.

Life-Changing Challenge: The Father/Mother or Household leaders should, along with the family, identify people within the family that need to give their lives to Jesus in baptism. Write their names down in the prayer journal and begin asking God for the courage to make an appeal to them to be baptized.

Day 30 "Ministry Project Prayer"

> **LIFE - CHANGING FAMILY WORSHIP FORMAT**
>
> SING • Sing a song(s) of praise that everyone can enjoy.
> PRAY • Pray for God's presence to fill every heart.
> BIBLE • Read short and brief text (Life-Changing Idea and Life-Changing Scripture) or a story from the Bible.
> SHARE • Have everyone share what they've learned as well as prayer requests and praise reports.

Life-Changing Scripture: "Therefore go and make disciples of all nations..." Matthew 28:19 NIV

Life-Changing Idea: Our family exists for the blessing of others and for the glory of God.

Life-Changing Challenge: Pray that God would reveal a family ministry project idea to the family today.

Day 31 "Ministry Project Selection"

> **LIFE - CHANGING FAMILY WORSHIP FORMAT**
>
> SING • Sing a song(s) of praise that everyone can enjoy.
> PRAY • Pray for God's presence to fill every heart.
> BIBLE • Read short and brief text (Life-Changing Idea and Life-Changing Scripture) or a story from the Bible.
> SHARE • Have everyone share what they've learned as well as prayer requests and praise reports.

Life-Changing Scripture: "Therefore go and make disciples of all nations..." Matthew 28:19 NIV

Life-Changing Idea: Families that plan ministry together stay together. Families must do more than pray together, they must actually fulfill purpose together.

Life-Changing Challenge: Have the family discuss and select a family ministry project that all can participate in.

Day 32 "Selection Day"

> **LIFE - CHANGING FAMILY WORSHIP FORMAT**
>
> | | |
> |---|---|
> | SING | • Sing a song(s) of praise that everyone can enjoy. |
> | PRAY | • Pray for God's presence to fill every heart. |
> | BIBLE | • Read short and brief text (Life-Changing Idea and Life-Changing Scripture) or a story from the Bible. |
> | SHARE | • Have everyone share what they've learned as well as prayer requests and praise reports. |

Life-Changing Scripture: "Therefore go and make disciples of all nations..." Matthew 28:19 NIV

Life-Changing Idea: The enemy desires to destroy purpose, especially in families. Foil his plans today. Prepare yourselves for what God wants to do in you today. For His Glory!

Life-Changing Challenge: Prayerfully select a day when your family will do the family ministry project.

Day 33 "Affirmation Day"

>> **LIFE - CHANGING FAMILY WORSHIP FORMAT**

SING	• Sing a song(s) of praise that everyone can enjoy.
PRAY	• Pray for God's presence to fill every heart.
BIBLE	• Read short and brief text (Life-Changing Idea and Life-Changing Scripture) or a story from the Bible.
SHARE	• Have everyone share what they've learned as well as prayer requests and praise reports.

Life-Changing Scripture: "Therefore go and make disciples of all nations…" Matthew 28:19 NIV

Life-Changing Idea: "Sticks and stones may break my bones but words will never hurt me," is one of the biggest lies ever told. Words can either bless or curse. They can hurt or heal. Choose as a family today to bless one another with your words. Don't just expect a blessing. Be a blessing!

Life-Changing Challenge: Share words of affirmation with everyone in the family at the family worship. See who can give the most affirmations.

Day 34 "Let's Eat! Together."

> **LIFE - CHANGING FAMILY WORSHIP FORMAT**
>
> SING • Sing a song(s) of praise that everyone can enjoy.
> PRAY • Pray for God's presence to fill every heart.
> BIBLE • Read short and brief text (Life-Changing Idea and Life-Changing Scripture) or a story from the Bible.
> SHARE • Have everyone share what they've learned as well as prayer requests and praise reports.

Life-Changing Scripture: "Therefore go and make disciples of all nations…" Matthew 28:19 NIV

Life-Changing Idea: A *Time* magazine article suggests that kids who dine with the folks are healthier, happier, and better students. Sitting around a table with family does more for your it's growth than sitting in front of the television.

Life-Changing Challenge: Plan to share a meal together at home this evening as a family after family worship.

Day 35 "Memory Lane"

> **LIFE - CHANGING FAMILY WORSHIP FORMAT**
>
> **SING** • Sing a song(s) of praise that everyone can enjoy.
> **PRAY** • Pray for God's presence to fill every heart.
> **BIBLE** • Read short and brief text (Life-Changing Idea and Life-Changing Scripture) or a story from the Bible.
> **SHARE** • Have everyone share what they've learned as well as prayer requests and praise reports.

Life-Changing Scripture: "Therefore go and make disciples of all nations…" Matthew 28:19 NIV

Life-Changing Idea: When you don't feel blessed. Pause. Reflect. Remember. Give thanks.

Life-Changing Challenge: Take a trip down memory lane or create a new memory by either taking some family pictures or looking through old photo albums and talking about them and the memories they represent.

Week 6

"A FAMILY THAT PRAYS"
Family Prayer

"Therefore go and make disciples of all nations..."
Matthew 28:19 NIV

Day 36 "Family Meeting"

>> LIFE-CHANGING FAMILY WORSHIP FORMAT

SING	• Sing a song(s) of praise that everyone can enjoy.
PRAY	• Pray for God's presence to fill every heart.
BIBLE	• Read short and brief text (Life-Changing Idea and Life-Changing Scripture) or a story from the Bible.
SHARE	• Have everyone share what they've learned as well as prayer requests and praise reports.

Life-Changing Scripture: "Therefore go and make disciples of all nations..." Matthew 28:19 NIV

Life-Changing Idea: Families must plan to succeed. This often means they must meet and talk about where the family is going. You cannot travel effectively without knowing your destination. As a family you need to meet periodically having "family discussions" about how you are doing as a family reaching your family goals. Don't just expect success. Plan for it. Talk about it. Pray for it. Experience it.

Life-Changing Challenge: Select a time weekly or monthly when the family will come together to meet about family business, such as the maintenance of the house, financial matters, ministry projects or other family matters.

Day 37 "Life-Changing Prayer"

> **LIFE-CHANGING FAMILY WORSHIP FORMAT**
>
> SING • Sing a song(s) of praise that everyone can enjoy.
> PRAY • Pray for God's presence to fill every heart.
> BIBLE • Read short and brief text (Life-Changing Idea and Life-Changing Scripture) or a story from the Bible.
> SHARE • Have everyone share what they've learned as well as prayer requests and praise reports.

Life-Changing Scripture: "Therefore go and make disciples of all nations..." Matthew 28:19 NIV

Life-Changing Idea: God works through prayer not independent of it. Prayer is the God's way of moving in your life. My friend Frank Wright says it like this, "I bow my knees. Lift my hands. Speak. Problem solved." It's just that simple. Either pray or worry, don't do both.

Life-Changing Challenge: Pray hard and earnestly for a family breakthrough for one person in the family who needs spiritual deliverance.

Day 38 "Life-Changing Prayer"

> **LIFE - CHANGING FAMILY WORSHIP FORMAT**
>
> | | |
> |---|---|
> | SING | • Sing a song(s) of praise that everyone can enjoy. |
> | PRAY | • Pray for God's presence to fill every heart. |
> | BIBLE | • Read short and brief text (Life-Changing Idea and Life-Changing Scripture) or a story from the Bible. |
> | SHARE | • Have everyone share what they've learned as well as prayer requests and praise reports. |

Life-Changing Scripture: "Therefore go and make disciples of all nations…" Matthew 28:19 NIV

Life-Changing Idea: God's plan for your life is most often connected with the pain in your life. There is no pain without purpose.

Life-Changing Challenge: Pray hard and earnestly for a family breakthrough in the area of family ministry. You are asking God to activate your family to fulfill God's purpose making disciples. Ask the family: "What is our unique ministry?"

Day 39 "Life-Changing Prayer"

LIFE - CHANGING FAMILY WORSHIP FORMAT

SING	• Sing a song(s) of praise that everyone can enjoy.
PRAY	• Pray for God's presence to fill every heart.
BIBLE	• Read short and brief text (Life-Changing Idea and Life-Changing Scripture) or a story from the Bible.
SHARE	• Have everyone share what they've learned as well as prayer requests and praise reports.

Life-Changing Scripture: "Therefore go and make disciples of all nations..." Matthew 28:19 NIV

Life-Changing Idea: The Holy Spirit is not a "thing" to be used, but he is the Divine Comforter that wants to use you!

Life-Changing Challenge: Pray hard and earnestly for a family breakthrough for total healing of the family, claiming that God would move specifically on tomorrow when you have your special family anointing service.

Day 40 "Anointing"

> **LIFE-CHANGING FAMILY WORSHIP FORMAT**
>
> | | |
> |---|---|
> | SING | • Sing a song(s) of praise that everyone can enjoy. |
> | PRAY | • Pray for God's presence to fill every heart. |
> | BIBLE | • Read short and brief text (Life-Changing Idea and Life-Changing Scripture) or a story from the Bible. |
> | SHARE | • Have everyone share what they've learned as well as prayer requests and praise reports. |

Life-Changing Scripture: "Therefore go and make disciples of all nations..." Matthew 28:19 NIV

Life-Changing Idea: You and your family's greatest need is to be filled with the Holy Spirit. The greatest evidence that you have the Holy Spirit living in your life is love (Read Galatians 5). No Spirit. No love. Everything your family needs in is receiving the Holy Spirit. The Holy Spirit brings the life and presence of Christ into your heart and home. In order for a person or a family to become like Jesus they must be filled or controlled by the Holy Spirit. Families need to understand that everything they need is in surrendering to the leading of the Spirit. There is one way to receive the Holy Spirit into your life and home-- ask. The Bible simply says, "So I say to you: Ask and it will be given to you; seek and you will find; knock and the door will be opened to you. For everyone who asks receives; the one who seeks finds; and to the one who knocks, the door will be opened" (Luke 11:9,10 NIV).

Life-Changing Challenge: The family leader should obtain some special olive oil and at the end of family worship anoint each family member on the forehead and have a season of prayer, praying that God would bless the family with the Holy Spirit and healing in every area of life.

After Worship: Go out to eat or have a special dinner to celebrate the 40 days of Life-Changing Family Worship. Have each member share testimonies of what the 40 days has meant to them.

A FINAL WORD

If you are reading this now, you probably have finished the 40 day Life-Changing Family Worship Challenge. I am confident that you have experienced a life change and have gained a fresh experience with God in your household and a powerful testimony. I want you to take a moment and reflect on what God has done for you over the last 40 days and journal about it below.

What Did God Do in Your House?

_____

_____

_____

_____

_____

NOTES:

NOTES:

NOTES:

NOTES:

NOTES:

NOTES:

NOTES:

NOTES:

Remember

Remember is the key word. Remember God everyday in your home. The day you forget God is the day you risk the spiritual security of your home. Cover your family each day with time in God's presence. This experience should have built family worship into the fabric of your lifestyle and routine. Whatever you do from this day forward, don't stop what you've started. Keep bringing your family into the presence of God. You are not by yourself. Your family has not been left to fend for themselves. Each day God is waiting you to bless you. The way to access His blessings is by continuing to come before Him as a household in worship.

"You will seek me and find me when you seek me with all your heart." Jeremiah 29:13 NIV

NOTES

introduction: **A Life-Changing Idea**
1. Matthew 18:19,20
2. Revelation 3:20
3. Ephesians 3:20

chapter 1: **My Story**
4. John 4:23,24

chapter 2: **The Purpose**
5. Ellen G. White, Child Guidance (Nashville: Southern Publishing Association), 518.

chapter 4: **2 Powerful Ideas**
6. Genesis 1:26
7. Revelation 14:6-12
8. Genesis 3:8

chapter 5: **The Solution: When God Shows Up**
9. Psalm 16:11
10. Mark 2:1-5
11. Luke 5:17

chapter 7: **What is Family Worship?**
12. Acts 2:42-45

chapter 8: **Getting Started: My Attitude**
    13.   Proverbs 23:7
    14.   John 6:37
    15.   Ephesians 4:15
    16.   Ephesians 3:20
    17.   Ephesians 6:18

chapter 9: **Getting Started: The Components**
    18.   Ephesians 5:19, 20
    19.   Psalm 34:1
    20.   Ellen G. White, Child Guidance (Nashville: Southern Publishing Association), 517.
    21.   Jeremiah 33:3
    22.   Psalm 119:105
    23.   Romans 10:17
    24.   Hebrews 11:6
    25.   Revelation 12:11
    26.   2 Corinthians 1:2
    27.   Proverbs 18:21
    28.   Ephesians 4:29
    29.   Proverbs 10:11
    30.   Philippians 4:13

OA.BLUEPRINTS

GRAPHIC DESIGN & WEB DEVELOPMENT

OA.Blueprints, LLC is a premier graphic design and web development company. We provide professional, high-quality, affordable design and web services to meet our clients' needs. Our clients appreciate the quality and creativity of our work, as well as our quick turnaround time on projects. For more information please visit www.oablueprints.com or contact us at 708-912-1112 or oablueprints@yahoo.com.

- Logo Design
- Corporate Branding and Identity
- Print Design
- Illustration
- Website Design and Development
- Book Cover Design and Interior Layout
- And much more...

SPIRIT REIGN
COMMUNICATIONS & PUBLISHING

A Message From Our Founder

Thank you for supporting our company. As we grow in grace, we hope and pray that you will continue to journey with us. We have many plans for the future, and without your support we will never reach our goals.

Spirit Reign Communications and Publishing was established to produce quality Christ-centered presentations in a variety of mediums. Our commitment to excellence is manifested in the published works, ministerial resource materials, goods and services we provide for our clients and customers. We have been blessed with an innovative team of visionary thinkers whose business and creative prowess distinguish us in a unique and positive way. Whether in traditional print, electronic format, or audio and visual recording, we effectively communicate the word of God in the 21st century with contemporary slants on the age-old gospel. Among the ministries we support, we are proud sponsors of Families At The Altar Ministries, The Prodigy Plan, and Jeremy Anderson Ministries. We also offer professional art and design services for the corporate identity of Christ-centered institutions.

Sincerely,

Daryl S. Anderson Sr.
Founder/CEO

"Our Family Is Your Family"

Order these and other great titles from our website www.spiritreign.org.

If There's An Author In You, Your Book Could Be Next

Take your first step toward a successful venture with Spirit Reign Publishing by visiting our website and pressing the publishing options tab. We're confident that you will appreciate our quality and dedication as we provide the best in faith based book publishing. Be blessed as you pen your potential best seller. Hope to see you soon.